Graceland

Ava Wong Davies

T0347993

methuen | drama
LONDON • NEW YORK • OXFORD • NEW DELHI • SYDNEY

METHUEN DRAMA
Bloomsbury Publishing Plc
50 Bedford Square, London, WC1B 3DP, UK
1385 Broadway, New York, NY 10018, USA
29 Earlsfort Terrace, Dublin 2, Ireland

BLOOMSBURY, METHUEN DRAMA and the Methuen
Drama logo are trademarks of Bloomsbury Publishing Plc

First published in Great Britain 2023

Cover design by Rebecca Heselton

Cover images: Kimson Doan/Michiel Annaert/Ethan Ridd/Sheng L/Unsplash

A catalogue record for this book is available from the British Library.

A catalog record for this book is available from the Library of Congress.

ISBN: PB: 978-1-3504-0927-9
ePDF: 978-1-3504-0928-6
eBook: 978-1-3504-0929-3

Series: Modern Plays

Typeset by Mark Heslington Ltd, Scarborough, North Yorkshire

To find out more about our authors and books visit
www.bloomsbury.com and sign up for our newsletters.

THE ROYAL COURT THEATRE PRESENTS

Graceland

by Ava Wong Davies

Graceland was first performed at the Royal Court Jerwood Theatre Upstairs, Sloane Square, on Thursday 9 February 2023.

Graceland
by Ava Wong Davies

Cast

Nina **Sabrina Wu**

Director **Anna Himali Howard**
Designer **Mydd Pharo**
Lighting Designer **Jai Morjaria**
Composer & Sound Designer **Anna Clock**
Associate Director **Jasmine Teo**
Production Manager **Juli Fraire**
Stage Managers **Rachel Rieley & Marie-Angelique St. Hill**

From the Royal Court, on this production:

Casting Directors **Amy Ball & Arthur Carrington**
Stage Supervisor **TJ Chappell-Meade**
Lighting Supervisor **Max Cherry**
Lead Producer **Sarah Georgeson**
Costume Supervisor **Katie Price**
Lighting Programmer **Stephen Settle**
Sound Supervisor **Jet Sharp**

Graceland is a co-production with SISTER.

Ava Wong Davies (Writer)

Theatre includes: Half Blue (Audible/LAMDA); Rime of the Second Sister (45North); I will still be whole (when you rip me in half) (Bunker).

Anna Clock

(Composer & Sound Designer)

Theatre includes: A Family Business (China Plate/Staatstheater Mainz); Kabul Goes Pop (Brixton House); Electric Rosary (Manchester Royal Exchange); The Beauty Queen of Leenane (Lyric Hammersmith); Crave (Chichester Festival); Speak Softly, Go Far (Digital; Abbey); Another Planet (Lakeside Arts); Mystery Trip (Nigel & Louise); [Blank] (also Lyric Hammersmith), Inside (Orange Tree); The Effect (English Theatre Frankfurt); Earthquakes in London (Guildhall School of Music and Drama); I Wanna Be Yours (Paines Plough/Tamasha/UK Tour/Bush); Not F**kin' Sorry, Shuck 'n' Jive, Soft Animals, Fabric (Soho); Groove, Looking Forward (BAC); Mary & Maria (Camden People's).

Anna Himali Howard (Director)

As director: Orpheus (Opera North); Kabul Goes Pop (Brixton House); I Stand for What I Stand On (Strike a Light & GYCA); Inside (Orange Tree); I Wanna Be Yours (Bush & UK tour); A Small Place, Albatross (Gate); BE Next Young Company (& European Theatre Festival), Yours Sincerely (& Vaults Festival).

As assistant/associate director: Small Island (National); Fleabag (International tour, prod. Soho & Drywrite); Othello (Sam Wanamaker); Paines Plough's Roundabout Season (Roundabout).

As theatremaker: Jane Anger (Yard Live Drafts); mahabharat/a (Camden People's); The Beanfield (Breach, Edinburgh Fringe, New Diorama & UK tour).

Jai Morjaria (Lighting Designer)

Theatre design includes: Othello (National); The Trials (Donmar); My Son's A Queer (But What Can You Do?) (Ambassadors/Garrick/Underbelly/Turbine); Chasing Hares (Young Vic); Wuthering Heights (St Ann's Warehouse/National/US Tour/Wise Children); Accidental Death of an Anarchist, Scissors (Sheffield); Cruise (Duchess); House of Ife, Lava (Bush); The Cherry Orchard (Yard Theatre/HOME); Cherry Jezebel (Liverpool Theatre); Birthmarked (Bristol Old Vic); I'll Take You To Mrs. Cole (Complicite); Big Big Sky, The Hoes (Hampstead); The Sorcerer's Apprentice (Northern Stage); Out of the Dark (Rose Theatre Kingston); Welcome Home, Shuck'n'Jive, Whitewash (Soho); Anansi the Spider (Unicorn); Glory (Duke's/Red Ladder); Cuzco (Theatre503); Losing Venice (Orange Tree); 46 Beacon (Trafalgar Studios with Rick Fisher); Out There on Fried Meat Ridge Road (White Bear/Trafalgar Studios 2); Acorn (Courtyard).

Awards include: WhatsOnStage Award for Best Off West End Production (My Son's A Queer), 2016 Association of Lighting Designer's ETC Award.

Mydd Pharo (Designer)

Theatre includes: I am Kevin, 100: UnEarth, Wolf's Child, The Great Survey of Hastings, A Great Night Out, The Cinema of Dreams, Twice Upon A Castle, Once Upon A Castle, The Yule-tide Ark-ive, 100: The Day Our World Changed, Nablus: City of Stories, Arkive, BABEL, Enchanted Palace (WildWorks); The Third Day (Punchdrunk /HBO/Sky Arts); I Wanna Be Yours (Paines Plough/Tamasha); Party Skills for The End Of The World (Assembly Hall/Shoreditch Town Hall); Hearty (Yard); Hansel Und Gretel (Royal College of Music); The Body (Barbican); The Wild Bride (Kneehigh/Lyric Hammersmith/The Asylum), The Passion (WildWorks/National Theatre Wales/Michael Sheen).

Rachel Rieley
(Stage Manager - Book)

As stage manager: The Wonderful World of Disscocia (Theatre Royal Stratford East); Dalia (Garsington Opera); Various Productions (Academy of Live and Recorded Arts); Summer Repertory Season (Frinton Summer Theatre).

As deputy stage manager: Shining City (Theatre Royal Stratford East); Jack and The Beanstalk (Theatre Royal Bath).

As assistant stage manager: Absurd Person Singular (Watford Palace Theatre); The Village (Theatre Royal Stratford East); Summer Repertory Season (Pitlochry Festival Theatre).

As props assistant: Summer Repertory Season 2022 (Garsington Opera); Two Ladies (Bridge); Hedda Tesman (Chichester Festival Theatre).

Marie-Angelique St. Hill
(Stage Manager - Props)

For the Royal Court: For Black Boys Who Have Considered Suicide When The Hue Gets Too Heavy.

As stage manager, other theatre includes: REP Season (Training) (National Youth); 5 Plays (Young Vic).

As assistant stage manager, for the Royal Court: A Kind of People.

As assistant stage manager, other theatre includes: Dirty Dancing (Secret Cinema); Hamlet, Tree (Young Vic/& MIF); Aladdin (Hackney Empire); In the night garden tour (Minor Entertainment).

Jasmine Teo
(Associate Director)

As director, theatre includes: **These Demons (Seven Dials); The Bevin Boys, The Art of Charlie Chan Hock Chye (Pentameters); The Gift (RADA); The Last Five Years (Henderson Project); Qibla (ArtsEd).**

As associate director, theatre includes: **A Christmas Carol (Nicholas Hytner, Bridge Theatre); A Christmas Carol (Nottingham Playhouse).**

As assistant director, theatre includes: **Jerusalem (Apollo); Camp Siegfried (Old Vic); The Haystack (Hampstead); The Wolves (Theatre Royal Stratford East), Company (Drama Centre); Il Ritorno d'Ulisse in Patria (Justin Way, Iford Music Festival); The Merry Widow (Esplanade).**

Awards include: **London Pub Theatres' Standing Ovation Award for Best New Play Raising Awareness 2019 (The Bevin Boys).**

Juli Fraire
(Production Manager)

For the Royal Court: A Fight Against...

Other theatre credits include: **A Christmas Carol...ish (Soho); Handbagged (Kiln); MIDDLE (National); Sundown Kiki (Young Vic); Psychodrama (Psycho Productions); Suzy Stork (Gate).**

Opera and musical credits include: **Betty Blue Eyes (Pimlico Opera); L'incoronazione di Poppea (Longborough Festival Opera); Effigies of Wickedness (Gate/ENO).**

Sabrina Wu (Nina)

Theatre includes: **The Doctor (Duke of York's); Screen 9 (Pleasance); A Respectable Wedding, Cherries in the Fall (La Mama).**

Radio includes: **United Kingdoms, Dark Harbour.**

THE ROYAL COURT THEATRE

The Royal Court Theatre is the writers' theatre. It is a leading force in world theatre for cultivating and supporting writers – undiscovered, emerging and established.

Through the writers, the Royal Court is at the forefront of creating restless, alert, provocative theatre about now. We open our doors to the unheard voices and free thinkers that, through their writing, change our way of seeing.

Over 120,000 people visit the Royal Court in Sloane Square, London, each year and many thousands more see our work elsewhere through transfers to the West End and New York, UK and international tours, digital platforms, our residencies across London, and our site-specific work. Through all our work we strive to inspire audiences and influence future writers with radical thinking and provocative discussion.

The Royal Court's extensive development activity encompasses a diverse range of writers and artists and includes an ongoing programme of writers' attachments, readings, workshops and playwriting groups. Twenty years of the International Department's pioneering work around the world means the Royal Court has relationships with writers on every continent.

Since 1956 we have commissioned and produced hundreds of writers, from John Osborne to Jasmine Lee-Jones. Royal Court plays from every decade are now performed on stage and taught in classrooms and universities across the globe.

We strive to create an environment in which differing voices and opinions can co-exist. In current times, it is becoming increasingly difficult for writers to write what they want or need to write without fear, and we will do everything we can to rise above a narrowing of viewpoints.

It is because of this commitment to the writer and our future that we believe there is no more important theatre in the world than the Royal Court.

🐦 royalcourt ⬛ royalcourttheatre

Supported using public funding by
**ARTS COUNCIL
ENGLAND**

ASSISTED PERFORMANCES

Captioned Performances

Captioned performances are accessible for people who are deaf, deafened & hard of hearing, as well as being suitable for people for whom English is not a first language.

Graceland: 3, 10 March 7.45pm
BLACK SUPERHERO: 12, 19 April 7.30pm, 27 April 2.30pm

BSL-interpreted Performances

BSL-interpreted performances, delivered by an interpreter, give a sign interpretation of the text spoken and/or sung by artists in the onstage production.

Audio-described Performances

Audio-described performances are accessible for people who are blind or partially blind. They are preceded by a touch tour which allows patrons access to elements of theatre design including set and cosutme.

Sound of the Underground: 25 February 2:30pm with TT at 1pm

BLACK SUPERHERO: 29 April 2:30pm with TT at 1pm

ASSISTED PERFORMANCES

Performances in a Relaxed Environment

Relaxed Environment performances are suitable for those who may benefit from a more relaxed environment.

During these performances:

- There is a relaxed attitude to noise in the auditorium; you are welcome to respond to the show in whatever way feels natural
- You can enter and exit the auditorium when needed
- We will help you find the best seats for your experience
- House lights may remain raised slightly
- Loud noises may be reduced

Graceland: 11 March 3pm

BLACK SUPERHERO: 22 April 2.30pm

If you would like to talk to us about your access requirements, please contact our Box Office at (0)20 7565 5000 or boxoffice@royalcourttheatre.com The Royal Court Visual Story is available on our website. Story and Sensory synopses are available on the show pages via the Whats On tab of the website shortly after Press Night.

ROYAL COURT SUPPORTERS

The Royal Court Theatre relies on the support we receive from individuals, trusts and corporate partners to help us to achieve our mission of supporting, nurturing and empowering writers at every stage of their careers. Through our writers, we are at the forefront of creating restless, alert, provocative theatre that reflects the world in which we live and our mission is more important than ever in today's world.

Our supporters are part of the essential fabric that enables us to keep our finger on the pulse – they give us the freedom to take bigger and bolder risks, challenge the status quo and create world-class theatre that affects and disrupts the theatre ecology. It is through this vital support that the Royal Court remains the writers' theatre and that we can continue to seek out, develop and nurture new voices both on and off our stages.

Thank you to all who support the Royal Court. We really can't do it without you.

ROYAL

BAR & KITCHEN

The Royal Court's Bar & Kitchen aims to create a welcoming and inspiring environment with a style and ethos that reflects the work we put on stage.

Offering expertly crafted cocktails alongside an extensive selection of craft gins and beers, wine and soft drinks, our vibrant basement bar provides a sanctuary in the middle of Sloane Square. By day a perfect spot for meetings or quiet reflection and by night atmospheric meeting spaces for cast, crew, audiences and the general public.

All profits go directly to supporting the work of the Royal Court theatre, cultivating and supporting writers – undiscovered, emerging and established.

For more information, visit
royalcourttheatre.com/bar

HIRES & EVENTS

The Royal Court is available to hire for celebrations, rehearsals, meetings, filming, ceremonies and much more. Our two theatre spaces can be hired for conferences and showcases, and the building is a unique venue for bespoke events and receptions.

For more information, visit
royalcourttheatre.com/events

Sloane Square London, SW1W 8AS ⊖ Sloane Square ⇄ Victoria Station
🐦 royalcourt 📘 theroyalcourttheatre 📷 royalcourttheatre

SUPPORT THE COURT AND BE A PART OF OUR FUTURE.

Every penny raised goes directly towards producing bold new writing for our stages, cultivating and supporting writers in the UK and around the world, and inspiring the next generation of theatre-makers.

You can make a one-off donation by text:

Text **Support 5** to 70560 to donate £5
Text **Support 10** to 70560 to donate £10
Text **Support 20** to 70560 to donate £20

Texts cost the donation amount plus one standard message. UK networks only.

To find out more about the different ways in which you can get involved, visit our website: royalcourttheatre.com/support-us

The English Stage Company at the Royal Court Theatre is a registered charity (No.231242)

Acknowledgements

Enormous thanks to:

Anna Himali Howard, Izzy Rabey, Sabrina Wu, Anna Clock, Mydd Pharo, Jai Morjaria, Juli Fraire Willemoes, Jasmine Teo, Katie Price, Marie-Angelique St. Hill, Rachel Rieley, Mica Taylor, Sarah Georgeson, and Arthur Carrington

Jessi Stewart

Lucy Morrison

Jane Fallowfield

Vicky Featherstone

Everyone at the Royal Court

Callan McCarthy and Methuen Drama

Eve Allin, Lulu Raczka, Sam Ward, Tom Hammond, lydia luke, Liv Wynter, Ben Schwarz, Tara Doolabh, and Joseph Fuller

The Ambassador Theatre Group x Platform Presents Playwriting Award

Emma Dennis-Edwards and the 2021 Royal Court Writers' Group

Graceland

'We made
the mistake of kissing there. I mean, here.'
Mid-Air, Caroline Bird

'It pains me to record this,
I am not a melodramatic person.'
The Glass Essay, Anne Carson

Character

Nina, *British Chinese woman, mid-20s*

Script Grammar

+   *indicates a shift in time or space.*
'   *suggests a beat of silence. Sometimes the length of a breath,
    sometimes longer.*

Italics are suggested actions.

*I have tried to put in 'I/you/they say' to make the speaker clear, but
these can and should be cut if needed.*

Line breaks are suggestive of rhythm, but it isn't an exact science.

This playscript may differ from the version performed.

Nina   We meet at a barbecue.

I meet you at a barbecue.

Which is perhaps not the most –

I wish we hadn't met there.

I wish I could say it was something more interesting, but unfortunately, the truth is, I meet you at an overly optimistic springtime barbecue while I have ketchup running down my chin and my face is ruddy from lukewarm beer and you –

Well.

You look like you.

Beautiful.

Sam hangs off Josh's arm while he pokes at the grill.

'Are you having fun? Who have you spoken to?'

The truth is that I've spent most of the last hour sitting in the bathroom, counting floor tiles.

'Lots of people.'

'As if.' Josh waggles his tongs at me like we're friends.

I hold up a hand to bat him away –

And it's then that I spot you.

You're standing there.

In the middle of a badly mown garden in Tooting.

Not talking to anyone.

Just standing.

I can't believe I didn't spot you before.

Sam follows my stare.

'I can introduce you. He's interesting.'

Josh snorts.

Sam and Josh met eighteen months ago at a ball pit cocktail bar. Sam and I used to laugh about the ball pit, but she doesn't think it's funny anymore.

So I'm bored, and the warmth of the beer curls somewhere here –

She touches her abdomen.

And so I say –

Yes.

Yes.

Yes please.

She calls your name –

And –

You turn.

And the evening light glances off your cheek and I am –

'

She introduces us with a bad joke and then she walks away.

I cross my arms, let them fall to my sides, cross them again.

You watch me.

I don't know how to –

'What?' I say, like a teenager.

'Nothing.'

I don't know what to do, so I reach out and take your cup and sip the sickly white wine.

'It's warm.'

You smile and you take it back, and you drink from the same spot where my lips were.

After a moment, you ask how I know Sam, and I tell you we went to school together.

You nod, slowly, like I've said something fascinating.

'What about you?' I say.

'University. We did the debate team.'

Of course.

I know you.

I have you all figured out.

'You were the free speech on campus type,' I say, suddenly bold.

You smile again, except there is a quizzical line between your brows.

'Is that what you think of me?'

I kick the ground. 'I don't know. I don't know you.'

You look at me, and I look away.

Then you say:

'You don't belong here. Do you?'

'

'What do you do?' I ask.

'I'm a poet,' you say, without a hint of irony.

I laugh, then stop.

'How can someone be a poet?'

'With considerable difficulty.'

You speak slowly, quietly.

I have to lean in to hear you.

Your shirt is Ralph Lauren, but it's wearing thin at the elbows.

'You look like a poet,' I say.

Now you laugh for the first time, and my whole body vibrates.

'You mean I look scruffy.'

'No, just –'

'Scruffy,' you say again.

'No. Well. In a nice way.'

'Oh, in a nice way.'

Again, that smile. God.

You ask me what I do, and I tell you I'm a receptionist.

'And do you like it?'

'I don't have an opinion on it,' I say, looking past your ear. You tilt your head at me, and a curl of hair dips into your eyes.

'What would you most want to do?' Your voice low. 'If you could do anything.'

'I don't know. Be a kept woman, maybe.'

You laugh again, and something uncoils.

I ask if you make money from being a poet, and you say that's a vulgar question.

I say that's what rich people say when they don't want to admit they're rich.

'Who says I don't want to admit it?'

You lead me into the kitchen, and you reach into the drinks cupboard and take out a bottle of good whisky.

'Don't.'

'We'll replace it.'

Half an hour later, I kiss you under fluorescent light.

You taste of smoke and something else.

A dull, damp, rich thing, like red wine spilled on carpet, like blood in your mouth.

In Sam's room, I lock the door behind us.

'Trapping me?' you say.

You go down on me, and I shut my eyes.

You stop and look at me.

'Are you uncomfortable?'

'No.'

'Your legs are tense.'

'No. I don't know.'

'You don't know?'

I throw my arm over my eyes. You sit up.

'You're self conscious?'

I want to scream, so I shake my head.

'We'll stop.'

You lie beside me and run your thumb over my lip, and I catch it between my teeth.

You kiss me and get up to leave, and I get the sense that I might never see you again, and so I say to you, as your hand reaches for the door:

'Take my number. Will you take my number?'

And you stop, and you turn to me, and you smile.

Just a little.

'Alright.'

'

Now, listen.

I didn't –

I don't –

Believe in love at first sight.

But it feels like I'm falling.

What else would you call that?

+

I suck my thumb until I'm nine.

My mum slaps my hand away from my mouth, appalled.

I stop eventually, but only so I can bite my cuticles until they bleed.

My parents run a restaurant on a once-busy London high street.

It has cracked neon lighting and the chefs spit into the alleyway.

Laminated family pictures peel off the walls.

The ovens shudder and groan.

I chew on the spare ribs the chefs save for me and race around the restaurant, hiding under tables and scaring customers.

My mum follows, tucking the phone under her chin, legs tangled in the cord.

She hauls me upstairs, smacking me with a coat hanger until I scream.

Afterwards, we sit and watch swooning Canto dramas together and she explains the plots to me.

'That one works too hard in the big city, and doesn't think she needs romance. Her boyfriend died many years ago, but now his twin brother has come to the city and is looking for money.'

She points out her favourite couples and instructs me to rub her feet.

'It's nice to pretend,' she says as I massage her arches.

Every evening, she sits by the counter, gossiping with her friend, a Malaysian woman who wears costume jewellery on her fingers and smokes constantly.

She ushers her son towards me.

Chris has cheeks like fresh dough, and hides behind her legs.

We eat eggs and rice on the floor with our legs splayed wide.

'Close your legs,' my mum tells me. 'And stop eating fish eyes. Don't scare the customers.'

'Okay,' I say, my face hot, and I stop.

When I'm ten, she saves up and enrols me in chess club, in piano lessons, in netball teams.

I end up too impatient for chess, too clumsy for piano, too slow for netball, so she stops after a year.

'Waste of money,' she says.

When we turn thirteen, the chefs start getting Chris to cut up onions. He does it slowly, methodically. I start taking orders, but the words stiffen in my mouth, so she grabs the phone and waves me away.

I sneak out during service to hang around the park.

By the swing sets, I meet a girl in the year above called Sam, who has thick black eyeliner and teaches me how to smoke.

I skive off waitressing, my mum calls me selfish in front of everyone, I shrug it off.

I get older, and she stops asking.

My father –

My father looks at me, then wipes his brow and calls service.

Some weeks I see him, other weeks he disappears.

I ask my mum about it when I'm sixteen, and she tells me not to ask stupid questions.

Her back is tight and hard when I crawl into bed with her on the nights that he's gone.

When I'm twenty, I get an office job and tell her I'm moving to Haringey, and it's the first time I see her cry.

In the new flat, I pick at my fingernails, and then stop when I remember.

Somehow, I do it in my sleep and wake up with bloody fingertips.

'

I cry a lot when I'm little.

My mum wipes my face with a rough flannel.

She hoists me onto her lap and gives me a black bean bao to eat, peeling off the rough shell, letting the steam escape.

'No more crying. Mummy loves you thousands, okay?'

When I'm eight, in the darkness of my bedroom, I learn to masturbate, though it'll be years before I can put a name to it.

I do it all the time, with a kind of terrible, focused intensity.

Like the world will end if I stop.

+

'Who is he?' I ask Sam, hangover sticky.

She sighs down the phone.

'Did you have sex in our room?'

'No.' Technically true. 'Is Josh with you?'

'We're replacing the sofa. Stains.'

She bumped into you last week. Flustered in the dairy aisle, she invited you along.

'He'd just broken up with his girlfriend.' My stomach dips. 'I felt bad. I haven't seen him since we graduated. He was so . . .' The air crackles. 'Impressive.'

You two were only paired up for a debate once. Sam stuttered in the closing remarks, hungover and under-prepared, and you swooped in. Your team won. Afterwards, she said: 'It was you. All you.' You stared at her placidly, putting your notes away. 'Team effort,' you said.

All I have heard are the words 'ex-girlfriend.'

I ask her for your ex's name and she groans, then gives it to me.

I Google her name. Her hair is limp, and I'm thrilled.

Sam hangs up because Josh wants her opinion on coasters.

I search your name and scroll your LinkedIn on a private browser.

You worked for a consultancy until last year.

I zoom into your picture and squint.

I look up 'average consultant salary.'

I look for your social media but everything is set to private.

I find a poem you wrote that got published.

I start reading it, but I feel so sick and breathless with anticipation that I have to stop.

You don't text, and it's fine.

The next day, I sit behind my desk, making lunch reservations for other people.

I work with a lot of older men who call me 'ma'am', either as some joke I don't understand or because they figure it's polite.

My boss, Adam, likes to tap on my desk and say things like 'well well well,' and 'now what are we going to do with you?'

He winks at me as he brings clients in and I feel sorry for him.

I look through his invitations, sending the majority to trash.

And then –

You've sent me a Facebook request.

Bizarre. Facebook?

A message from you, immediately.

'Drink?' it says.

+

On a bench in Clissold Park, you tell me about your father.

He was away a lot for work, and I tell you I could have guessed, and you laugh, thank God.

'It's always either not enough love, or too much of it, or something in between,' you say.

Your father built tall apartment buildings in East London in the 90s.

You tell me he thinks your writing is interesting, and if he finds your career move disappointing, he won't say.

You do copy-editing for smoothie brands and insurance companies when you're not writing.

I say, 'That's interesting,' and you look at me and say, 'Is it?' and I laugh.

'What about you?' you say. 'Who are you?'

'

At the restaurant, you serve me first.

'Did you give me a fake number?' you ask, licking sauce off your thumb.

'No. Why?'

You show me a number with too many zeroes in it.

I cover my face. 'How drunk was I?'

Eventually, we tell that story at parties and learn when to pause for laughter.

Feeling brave, I ask about your ex, and you look amused.

'Been busy?'

'I have to do background checks.'

'Of course. For your safety.'

You tell me it ended because she cheated on you.

Pure relief.

The bill comes, and I offer to split, and you refuse, and I offer again, and then you relent, and we split.

In a cab, I watch you talk intently, animatedly, with the driver.

'What?' you say, when we get out.

'Nothing.'

'I thought he was interesting. Didn't you?'

My face is warm. 'I guess.'

You live in a flat in a terraced house off the side of Victoria Park.

'Belongs to my dad,' you say as you let me in. 'Yes, I know.'

'I didn't say anything.'

'Well, you have a very readable face.'

Now I think you might be nervous.

My hands drift over burnished, mid-century wood.

'I've always wanted a rocking chair.'

It was your grandmother's. You point at the sea glass on the mantelpiece. 'We'd go to the beach together when my parents were away.'

For some reason, this makes me want to take you into my arms.

Lay your head on my lap.

You place your hand on the inside of my thigh.

Carefully.

Afterwards you trace circles on my bare shoulder and it feels so intimate I could scream.

+

Then you go on holiday.

Every day for a week, I check the weather in Tallinn.

Three weeks of silence, then you text at 1 am on a Tuesday to ask me how I am.

We talk for a day, then I stop replying.

A week later, I go to a gig I know you'll be at.

You find me and kiss me against the bar.

I have a small bruise on my hip the next day.

I press on it.

Watch it go from yellow to purple.

You text me as I'm falling asleep.

'I want to see you properly. No more games.'

+

You meet my parents.

Chris nods from behind the counter but doesn't say hello, too busy carving duck into glistening pieces.

My mum piles food onto your plate.

You ask questions about the business and listen carefully as she speaks.

You talk about how one of your favourite Chinese restaurants was bought out.

'It's so sterile now. There's no character anymore.'

My mum says yes, exactly, that's exactly the problem.

My father watches you and drinks his beer.

Your eyes flit over him, and you make leading comments in his direction, but he doesn't bite.

He pretends his English is worse than it actually is.

You don't notice, but it embarrasses me.

After a few minutes, you take your losses.

'So, tell me,' you say to my mum, your arm resting on the back of my chair. 'When's she taking over?'

I tear the cuticle off my thumb.

'She won't,' my father says.

He doesn't elaborate, just takes another sip and turns to check on the chefs.

'She doesn't want to do it,' my mum says. 'It's okay. It's hard.'

You stroke the back of my hand with your index finger and I shake my head, just a little.

You start talking about a childhood holiday to Hong Kong, and a dish you ate there.

'It was like a cake, but savoury. I think they fried it and steamed it?'

'Lo bak go,' my mum says, relieved. 'Turnip cake. I will make it for you. Next time.'

I lean over to my father and speak in Cantonese.

'Why don't you say anything?'

He shrugs a little. Doesn't look at me.

In English, he says, 'Nice man. Well done.'

He finishes his beer. He gets up, apologises to you, says he has to get back to the kitchen.

You shake his hand.

He leans down to clap me on the shoulder, and as he does so, he asks me in Cantonese: 'Are you happy?'

'I've never been happier,' I say.

I mean it.

+

Sam invites us over for dinner.

You lean back in your chair in this particular way, and out of the corner of my eye, I see Josh adjusting himself, trying to mirror you, and it makes me laugh so much I hiccup.

While we're eating, I trip over my words and enunciate too much to make up for it, and everyone raises their eyebrows.

'She's a sloppy drunk,' you say to everyone except me.

Sam laughs like she didn't spend her teenage years with her head inside a toilet bowl.

Josh pretends to wrestle the wine bottle out of my hand, and something hot and sour rises up my chest.

I say, loudly, 'No I'm not,' and I swipe for the bottle, except that in this case, you are right, I am a sloppy drunk, and it smashes on the floor.

'Oh,' Josh says.

I get onto my hands and knees to pick up the pieces.

'Stop,' you call from behind me. 'You'll cut yourself.'

'Just sit down,' Sam says, moving towards the kitchen. 'I've got it.'

I shake my head, vision blurring.

Glass slices into my palm.

'Jesus. Are you alright?' Josh rises from his seat.

'Obviously not,' you say, the loudest I've heard you speak.

In the bathroom, you stem the flow with toilet paper and I twist away from you.

'Don't fuss,' I say. 'I don't need you to fuss over me.'

You don't reply, just dab the cut, and I'm humiliated.

So I say:

'Can you fuck off?'

And I push you away, as hard as I can.

Which isn't particularly hard, but –

And you don't stumble, but you do stop what you're doing.

'Sit down.'

'I'm fine.'

'Just sit down.'

I sit down.

You take my hand and give me a wad of toilet paper.

'Hold that against it,' you say. 'It isn't deep. You'll be fine.'

'I'm sorry.'

You don't reply, just reach for the door.

'I'm sorry,' I say again.

You stop, and turn back, and look at me.

(*Mildly.*) 'Don't be silly. It's just a cut. I told you to stop drinking.'

'Are you alright?' Sam says outside.

I push past her. 'It isn't deep.'

'Are you sure?'

Josh calls out, 'The fallen warrior returns,' and I laugh.

I turn back to ask you something, and Sam is looking at you, and you are looking at me, and for a moment, both your faces are unreadable.

+

There was a cliff on the horizon.

I didn't know, but then again, maybe I did, and I just didn't want to look.

+

We go swimming in the sea.

You go too far out, and my feet kick out into nothing.

'Wait,' I call.

You turn and wave.

I wrap my arms around your neck, and you hold my thighs, and we stay there, suspended.

'I love you,' I say.

You say it back, and the sky collapses in.

+

When you let me read your work, I have to keep one eye closed, like I can't look directly at it.

It scares me a little.

What you're able to see.

You submit to magazines, to literary journals.

You get into a lot of them. You get commissioned. You get your work read on the radio.

You have to pay money to submit to some awards, which I find strange.

'It's more about exposure.'

'You're plenty exposed.'

'Well, you don't get it.'

'Well, what's there to get?'

You pretend not to hear me and turn the page of your book.

You're keen for me to write.

One day, you buy me a journal.

Smooth, pebbled leather, monogrammed with my initials.

You tell me to write for ten minutes.

Doesn't matter about what.

And I try, I promise I do try, but I find it impossible.

I sit there, and I hold the pen, and there is this pressure inside me that is –

'I can't do it,' I tell you later.

'Well, that's not true,' you say. 'You just don't want to.'

'

The thing is, I like that you know more about it than me.

I like it when you tell me about things.

About rhyme schemes, syntax, metre.

I do. I'm sorry.

'

One night, when the wine we've drunk has settled and you're stroking my cheek, I say, 'Do you write about me?'

A pause, and then you say: 'No.'

I pull away. You squint at me.

'Why? Do you want me to?'

'No,' I say, and I'm not sure if I'm lying.

'Don't lie.'

'I thought all poets wrote about love.'

You start to grin.

'So you want to be my muse?'

'No,' and again, I don't know if I'm lying.

You wait. I can feel my tongue in my mouth.

'I'm not that self-centred.'

'Really? Everyone is.'

'I'm not.'

You hold your hands up. 'Okay.'

I say it doesn't matter, forget it, but you lean forward.

'Does it really matter to you?'

I cover my eyes. 'Please, oh my God.'

'Why do you care?'

It comes out before I realise. 'Did you write about your ex?'

There's silence, then you scoff a bit. Lean back. Say nothing.

'That's a yes,' and now it's like someone else is speaking. 'But not me.'

It's like you're looking at me for the first time. 'I didn't know you were so immature.'

It stings, but my mouth still moves, and my voice still rings out.

'I'm not immature.'

'Really?'

You get up. Brush your trousers off.

'I don't care,' I say. 'I just don't know why you're so opposed to it.'

'I don't ever think about it.'

You turn, so I reach out for your arm –

And –

You knock my hand away.

Hard.

I drop my hand, not because –

Not out of –

Not because it hurts, because it doesn't hurt.

Just out of –

It's odd.

'

You knock my hand away.

With your hand, you push –

Hard.

Without looking at me, you do it.

And the air changes.

'

It is almost something to be concerned about, but then again, it's almost just a push.

I've pushed you before.

The moment flutters, then settles.

The place where you touched me burns a little.

You still don't look at me, but your ears are pink.

+

I don't know how much money you have, but you wear it like a coat.

You rarely stay at my place.

You tell me that the flat is a hovel, which is true.

Sometimes I come home to find our landlord looking through the kitchen cupboards.

She refuses to replace my bed frame, which is splintered and lopsided.

I tell you offhand, and then I open my bank account a few days later to find that you've sent me £300.

'You can't do this.'

'It's just a loan,' you say, not even looking up.

So I buy a new bed frame.

I spend a lot of time in John Lewis running my hands over smooth metal.

You never ask for the money back.

A few months later, you ask me to move in with you.

I say yes, obviously, of course, please, yes.

I leave the bedframe in the old flat.

I don't pay you rent, and we split the bills.

We never talk about it, exactly. It just happens.

Your generosity is confusing.

You ask me to pay you back for coffees we had two months ago, smoothing the receipts out to show me the exact difference.

But when I smash my phone, you pay to fix the screen, ignoring my protests.

We're both drunk one night and we argue next to an ATM when I try to give you money.

I stuff notes into your hands. 'I don't want to owe you anything.'

Your face closes off and you hold your hands up, like you're warding me off.

'This is disgusting. Stop it.'

'It's not, I want us to be equal.'

You step back and let the money drop to the floor.

'I won't be part of this –'

'Just take it.'

'– Of whatever fucked up guilt you have. Don't involve me. I'm not interested.'

You walk off, and I scrabble for the notes on my knees.

'

Obviously, there are problems.

I'm not naive enough to think there wouldn't be.

You can be –

Standoffish.

Cold.

I can be clingy and nasty.

I'll pick a fight and it'll be deliriously exciting, and then you'll go quiet and shake your head, and I'll clutch at you.

'

I'd let you walk on top of me, if you wanted.

You know that.

+

At parties of people we halfway know, we hide ourselves in corners, talking low like we're the only people in the world.

You turn up in old woollen jackets with buttons falling off, shoes scuffed.

I kiss you in front of people, in a way that makes them look at their feet and makes you laugh into my open mouth.

We watch Josh talking, gesturing so much that his wine runs down the side of his glass.

'Do you think he can put his socks on without falling over?' You say it in this curling way, like I'm in on the joke, and I laugh despite myself, and you're pleased, so I'm pleased.

Sam, standing in the kitchen, turns to look at us, and I cover my face, but she knows.

I don't know how, but she does.

Her mouth, wet and open, like a wound.

And then you wind your arm around my waist and murmur something else, something about the way Josh pours wine, and I laugh again.

I like looking at you look at me.

You run your hand under my skirt when we get home, and I gasp when you bury your head in my collarbone.

I like feeling you here.

She places one hand on her chest, one on her stomach.

Right here.

I can feel every part of me when I'm pressed against you.

+

I meet your friends.

They're nice.

Genuinely.

They buy me drinks and they ask me questions and they listen to the answers.

You, drunker by the second, sling your arm over my shoulder.

One of them asks what I do, and I tell them, and they nod, and as I speak, you nestle your nose into my ear. I push you away.

'She's undervalued,' you say. 'She could be doing much more.'

One of your friends nods his head in sympathy. 'Bad management?'

Something curdles in my stomach and I say, 'It's fine. I don't really have any ambitions.'

They all smile like I've made a joke.

I go outside and one of them follows me out.

He rolls me a cigarette, and we smoke in silence, and after a moment he says, 'Sorry. He can get a bit, you know.'

He stops speaking, and I want to say no, I don't know.

Back inside.

You, drunk.

I get quieter and quieter.

We walk home and you stop in the middle of the street and cover your eyes and you say, 'I'm sorry. Oh I'm sorry.'

'For what?'

You shake your head. 'I love you so much.'

Then you throw up on the pavement.

I rub your back and I want to hit you.

+

I change the printer ink at work.

Adam comes over to check his schedule, and I tell him that I can't check it right now Adam, because I'm changing the printer ink.

He hovers.

'I wanted to ask you about something.'

'Okay.'

He says he wants to encourage my creative side, which I wasn't aware that I had.

All I want to do is lie in bed with you.

He leans towards me like he's going to tell me a secret, and then he asks me to design an invitation for a networking event.

He stands, wide legged, arms wrapped around himself, and rocks back and forth.

'You have an eye for that kind of thing.'

I wonder what I've done to make him think that.

I say all the right things anyway, that I won't let him down, that I'm grateful for his belief in me, and he looks genuinely happy, and despite myself, part of me is pleased.

I go to move past him.

And he reaches out and rests his hand on my lower back.

You're lying on the sofa. 'You're going to say that he brushed your back?'

I'm in the doorway. I shrug.

You sit up. 'I'm not saying it's not bad.'

'No, I know.'

'But you can see what they might say.' Your eyes are soft. 'Are you alright?'

I take off my coat. 'I just know what I felt.'

'And what was that?'

'I don't know,' I say, and we both laugh.

I lie down next to you and you wrap your arms around me.

In my ear, you say: 'Can you pick up your clothes? You left them on the floor again.'

Then –

'Why not quit? If you hate it so much.'

Part of me sings with joy.

And yet –

'Don't say that.' I sit up.

'Why? I could support you.' You stretch, yawning. 'I thought that's what you wanted. You could retrain.'

'But I don't know what I would train for.'

'To do something you care about?'

I hide my face in my hands.

'Don't be lazy.'

I look down at you, hair in my eyes. 'What?'

You are looking at me, unblinking. 'I love you. But you could be doing so much more. You know it's true.'

'

The next day, I buy lace underwear on my lunch break.

I change in the bathroom and feel it rubbing against my hip.

Adam waves from across the office, and I wave back.

I go home and you run it through your hands.

'New?' you say.

+

At the wedding of a girl I used to work with, I'm restless, excitable.

You're bored, and you think the marquee is tacky, and you have spent most of your time drinking whisky at the bar.

Bad whisky, you take pains to tell me how absolutely terrible this whisky is.

I scrunch up a cocktail napkin and throw it at you, and it bounces off your forehead and you go red and quiet, and I laugh and walk away.

I talk to one of the groomsmen for a little too long.

We do a shot together and I lick the salt from his wrist.

And then I look around to see if you've seen, and I catch your eye from across the dancefloor, and –

You look at me with such –

Disgust.

And something else.

All twisted up with it.

Just for a second.

And then it's gone.

'

So I leave him and I rush to you and I kiss the side of your face, the corner of your lip.

I pull you onto the dance floor, and for a moment, you try, you do try.

We do an awkward waltz and I stumble into your arms and my heel nearly breaks underneath me.

'Okay, enough.' You prop me up by the shoulders.

So I say: 'Fuck off.'

You release, and I nearly fall, and you leave the dancefloor and I don't see you for the rest of the night.

I fall into a pond, which makes all the people I don't know laugh, and I laugh too, and then I wake up in the morning outside the marquee with mud caked on my legs.

You stand over me, holding a bottle of water.

You take a baby wipe and clean my legs while I choke vomit into the flowerbeds.

'Up we get,' you say, gentle as anything, and we hobble to the car.

You make sure I don't bump my head and I sit in the front seat, head crackling, cheeks bruised with ruddiness.

You sit next to me, resting your head against the window.

Flies buzzing.

I can hear people stirring in the distance.

The smell of meat cooking, somewhere.

I pick at my fingernails.

(*Neutrally.*) 'Don't do that again,' you say.

'

I can see the bride waving from the marquee, holding a sandwich, ketchup running down her arm.

We wave back.

'Yes.'

+

Gradual, and then sudden.

+

It's busy when I arrive.

I see my mum apologising for late service in a voice that sounds unlike her own.

'Where have you been?' she says as I pass by. 'Three weeks and nothing? What if I died?'

I go out back.

Chris is there, smoking, his apron covered in dark splatters.

'You look disgusting,' I say.

'Yeah, what's new?'

I take his cigarette and we pass it back and forth.

'How's your mum?'

He glances at me. 'Oh, she's super chill nowadays.'

'Really?'

'No, idiot, she's insane.'

I laugh. He shakes his head, smiling.

'She always asks after you, you know.'

I blow smoke under orange light.

'Meg?' I ask.

He waves his hand and ash flies everywhere.

'It's over?'

'For months, man.'

'You're kidding.'

'You just haven't been here.'

He says this levelly, but his eyes flick towards me.

I notice a little hole in my trousers.

'Can you blame me?' I say, putting my finger through and pulling.

He shakes his head. 'They're alright.'

'You're not their daughter.'

'No, I guess not.' He pulls on the cigarette. 'How's your guy? Your fella?'

'My fella,' I roll the word around my mouth. 'You know, we moved in together.'

'Congratulations.'

He wipes his hands on his apron.

'Can I ask you something?'

'Of course.'

'How come we never, you know. Dated or whatever. It's not a big deal, it's just interesting to me.'

'

There is a light sheen of sweat on his forehead.

He folds his arms, coughs.

'Mum asked me a few weeks ago. I thought it was funny.'

'

'Why would you ask me that?'

'It's not a big deal.'

'I don't know why.'

'Okay,' he says, and he smiles.

'I don't.'

'I'm not trying to date you. It was just, I don't know. A question.'

He crushes the cigarette under his heel.

'You haven't even spoken to him,' I say. 'I tried to introduce you and you said you were too busy.'

'Yeah, because I was busy.'

'Too busy to say hello?'

'Too busy running this place.'

I go back inside.

My mum watches me come in and says nothing. Chris sends over crab soup but doesn't come over.

At home, I tell you what happened.

You stroke my cheek.

'Have you only ever dated white men?' you say.

+

We drive to meet your parents.

They live in a house in the countryside.

I look it up, and it is quite clearly more than a house, but you said house, so I say house too.

You're driving, because I'm a bad driver.

You hate that I say that about myself.

'It's a stereotype,' you say, and I want to ask what stereotype you mean, but I don't, I just smile, and you roll your eyes and get into the driver's seat.

We sing Paul Simon on the motorway and the sun breaks through cloud cover.

Your phone goes off, and you ask me to check it.

It's an email from an awards panel. You've won a prize. I tell you and you smile, only a little. So I tell you it's amazing, and you shake your head, and so I tell you again.

You say: 'These things are never really about talent.'

I say: 'They're a bit about talent.'

Then you look at me sideways.

'Really?'

You look back at the road, and then you look at me again.

'How would you know?'

'Well. I don't. You know your industry better than me.'

'What did you like about that one? You read it.'

I think about it.

I can't help but notice that you've sped up.

'I liked how it made me feel.'

You laugh.

'And what was that?'

I shrug and fiddle with the radio.

Static.

You tap the steering wheel with your thumb. One, two, three times.

'What do you think? Really. I want to know.'

I open my mouth and nothing comes out.

You laugh a bit, again.

'At least try,' you say.

'I don't know. It was just a feeling.'

'So rationalise it. Or tell me what the feeling was. You're not actually saying anything.'

Your voice doesn't rise.

The car in the next lane honks loud and long and you jerk away.

'Are you scared?'

'No.'

'You're gripping the seat.'

'I'm not,' I say, releasing.

The trees whip past.

Still, faster.

'You said I didn't deserve it.'

I comb through the conversation.

'I don't really know what we're arguing about.'

The car rattles.

'Can you slow down?'

Your shoulders are relaxed.

You take one hand off the wheel.

(*Neutrally.*) 'We're going to be late because you spent so long packing.'

You're right.

I couldn't decide between two shirts.

You were calling for me and I stood in our bedroom, and I held one in each hand, weighing them up.

In the end, I didn't bring either.

You overtake someone and the car swerves, and I can't think of what to do, so I say, 'Please don't crash. This is a rental.'

You laugh at me, and for one unreal second I laugh too.

And then I sit there and I think –

How did I let this happen?

Twenty minutes later, you pull into your parents' gravel drive and walk out of the car with the bags, leaving me there.

I think about sliding into your seat and reversing out.

Just driving.

Just road and sky.

Flying.

'

What if this is what it means?

To be loved?

If there's nothing else, at least there's feeling.

Sensation.

'

'Are you coming?' you call.

You're checking your watch, but your voice has softened.

'

Your mother fusses around the house like a bird caught indoors, opening and shutting cupboards, trying to find a salad bowl.

You drink a glass of water at the sink and catch her as she passes, planting a kiss on her cheek. She flaps her hands at you.

I massage kale for her, and she reaches over to squeeze my waist and says, 'We're going to be very good friends, I can just tell.'

Your father shuffles around in threadbare slippers. You and him talk parallel about the same topics.

He shows me around the house and tells me about visiting Beijing in the 90s.

When you mention the award offhand, he says to me, 'Now isn't that something!' and I say yes, yes, isn't it.

I walk in on you two sitting together by the fireplace, heads bent over the same book. You both look up at me, and it's uncanny.

We eat rigid cuts of meat in the dining room, and when I speak, I trip over my words and say things like 'anyway' and 'you know' and your father papers over the pauses with funny anecdotes and I can't think of anything to say back, and so eventually they just direct their words to you. I look down at the skin peeling off my thumb, red and raw, and I want to bite it.

In your bedroom, we crawl under itchy blankets.

You put on your glasses, and I reach over and lay my head on your chest.

You ignore me.

I splay my palm over your heart.

You ignore me.

I nestle my head into your armpit and wrap my arm around your torso.

You shift, and look down.

'What do you want?' you say, not unkindly.

I climb into your lap and kiss you.

You push me off.

I try again.

We take each other's clothes off carefully, and then quickly.

You flip me over, onto my back, and I cling to you.

There is this heat, this pressure, right here.

She touches her lower abdomen.

'Can you get a condom?' You roll off me.

'I don't think I have any here.' Your voice is rough, rising out of the darkness.

'Oh.'

You pull off your socks on the edge of the bed.

'I thought you wanted to go on the pill?'

'I dunno.' I lie there, suddenly shy. 'I don't really like it.'

You climb back onto the bed, and it creaks, and you freeze on all fours, naked and ridiculous, and we start giggling.

You come towards me and I pretend to push you away.

'You're freezing.'

'Come here.'

I say: 'I'll scream.'

'Go on.' You burrow your head into my neck and I kiss your hair.

'Did you hear your dad asking me about Beijing?' I say.

You groan. 'Don't talk about my dad right now.'

You move to lie on top of me and you kiss me.

You place your chin on my chest and smile, lazy, puppyish.

You kiss me again.

Warm now, and heavy.

'We should use a condom,' I say into your ear, hands clasped around the back of your neck.

Something like that.

I don't know.

I think I say something like that.

And then you push yourself inside me.

'

And it's not that it's painful, exactly.

'

I don't say anything.

Almost immediately, it feels good.

'

This is the thing I –

The part I find –

Because I spend weeks looking it up.

Typing out variations.

Different phrasings.

Nothing is quite –

'

I am aware of what you might call it.

'

Here's what I know.

After a moment, it starts to feel good –

I feel good.

That's what I feel.

'

At the same time.

It's just like I'm not there.

'

Afterwards.

In the morning, your parents leave, and you stroke my hair. 'What do you want to do? We could do anything.'

You make omelettes, soft and streaked with white, and we eat them in the garden, my feet on your lap.

You run me a bath and sit on the side.

'I love you,' you say, your chin resting on porcelain, your hand drifting in the water, and I believe it, I believe it, I believe it.

+

A few nights later, I kiss you, messy and wet, and when you're inside me, I hold you there.

The next night, I do it again.

On the third night, you shake your head.

'Maybe not tonight.' I have this hot fear in my chest and I paw at you until you reach for my waist.

I get the coil inserted, and I bleed for three weeks.

You warm up heating pads and place them on my stomach.

And then, you know, after that, it's fine.

'

You can be cruel.

So can a lot of people.

People are hard to love.

That's what makes it worth doing.

Love is something that requires patience, hard work, pain, which is what I tell myself when you ignore me, when you leave the room as I speak, when you refuse to look at me.

+

Sam is pale.

'Been ages.' Her smile is fixed and enormous.

She taps her spoon on the table and looks somewhere above my head.

I'm tired, irritable, and I say: 'What?'

She smiles again, that same smile, not looking at me. 'Just feel like I never see you anymore.'

'I'm busy.'

Now she eyes me.

'With what?'

'Work?'

'Okay,' she says, with the edge of a scoff.

I see myself, distorted and ugly in the mirror behind her.

I look at her. 'Your skin is grey.'

She leans back in her chair and fixes her eyes on her cup, and I think she might cry, but she doesn't.

It spills out of me. 'Are you sick? You should get some rest. Honestly, you look terrible.'

Her mouth tightens, but she says nothing.

We finish our coffees, she pays for both of us, and we hug at the station.

You're at the hob, stirring a pot.

'Don't you find her boring?'

I stand in the middle of the kitchen, adrift.

'Not really.'

You glance at me. 'My love, sit down.'

'I'm alright.'

You wipe your hands. 'It's normal to outgrow people.'

'We haven't outgrown each other,' I say, insistent.

You shrug. 'Okay.'

'We haven't.'

'Okay.' You start to plate up. 'I don't think she's my biggest fan, to be honest. We never have much to talk about.'

I stare out the window at nothing.

'I don't really care if she doesn't like me,' you say. 'Honestly, I don't think about her at all.'

+

My father and I drink beers in the living room.

The sofa sags when I sit on it.

'Just replace it,' I say in Cantonese.

He dismisses this with a wave of his hand.

He turns on the TV and we watch the news.

'Terrible,' he says about something terrible.

He checks his watch.

I check my phone.

After a moment, he turns to me. 'Your boyfriend. He's rich, no?'

I pause, and then I say, 'Yes.'

'That's good,' he says, nodding his head.

We both look at the TV.

And then I say: 'Where did you go?'

He shifts in his seat.

'When? I'm here.'

'When I was little,' I say, and the words stick. 'You'd go away. There were nights you weren't here.'

He shakes his head, still looking at the screen.

'I don't think so.'

'No, I remember it.'

I reach out to take his hand, and he grimaces a little.

In English, he says, 'You made that up,' and the pain is scalding, but I barrel through in quick Cantonese.

'What was it? The casino? Or somewhere else? Did you have a girlfriend?'

Still in English, he says, slowly, 'I don't think you remember it correctly.'

I wait.

He adjusts in his seat and the lamp light falls on his face.

He looks very old.

He turns the TV off. Sits there.

Cantonese again: 'You wouldn't understand. Your mother and I didn't know each other very well when we got married. It was –' And he pauses. 'Hard.'

'It was hard.'

He shrugs.

'So you left.'

He gets up and glares at me. 'Don't be dramatic.'

Then he sits back down.

I turn the TV back on.

We watch it for a while.

'I need to tell you something,' he says.

Surely he knows.

If he knows, then –

'Chris is becoming manager,' he says. 'We're getting too old. Your mother needs to rest.'

I knew, but it still comes out. 'But you never asked me.'

He looks at me with something close to pity.

He takes my empty bottle and rolls it around in his hands. 'Your boyfriend supports you, no?'

I want him to ask.

If he asks, I will tell him.

He just has to ask.

'Dad,' I say.

'What?'

His eyes run up and down my face, and then away.

In English, he says: 'I'm glad you're happy.'

+

At work, Adam leans over me to check the invitations.

'Lovely.' He squeezes my shoulder.

I shrug, just a little.

'Sorry,' he says automatically, stepping back.

You're sitting by the window. 'I told you to report him.'

Did you? I think.

You come and sit next to me, wrap your arm around my shoulders.

'It's not really a big deal,' I say, and it feels like the truth. 'I don't think it matters, really.'

'What are you talking about?'

I take your hand and twist my fingers through yours.

Absently, stupidly: 'You don't get it.'

The air moves, and you drop my hand.

'Whatever, then.'

'

'Sorry,' I say. 'I'm tired.'

You push away from the table.

'Hey,' I say.

Nothing.

I steady myself, settle my voice.

'Please.'

You blink and for a moment, you look at me with something like kindness. 'I don't know why you do this.'

And then you move towards the door, and then I know –

If you get to the bedroom, then this evening is over.

I reach out for your hand, but you pull away, already moving so quickly.

So I run to the door and I throw myself in front of it in a way which would feel melodramatic if it wasn't all so stupid anyway.

'Don't.' I try to catch your eye, try to make you look at me again.

'Please move.'

You reach around me and I go to block the handle –

And without a pause, you push me away from you, and I bump into the wall.

Hard, off-kilter.

You still don't look at me, just open the door.

So I rush to grab it before it closes and it shuts on my fingers.

I shout.

You come out, stare at me cradling my hand.

'Is it broken?' you say, your voice thick.

'I don't think so.'

A moment, a breath.

You look at me, finally.

And I reach out and I hit you in the face.

'

It leaves a red mark.

You touch your cheek, then put your hand down.

Something crosses your face.

Then you come towards me and I flinch.

I can't believe it.

You don't seem to notice, or maybe you just ignore it.

But you reach out and take my hand with outrageous tenderness.

'Stay here.'

Where else am I supposed –

You come back with frozen peas wrapped in a towel.

You ice my hand.

The mark on your face is already fading.

'We have to be more careful,' you say.

+

The doorbell rings and I open it.

You are behind me, and I can feel your breath on my neck.

My face is red from where I have spent the last ten minutes asking you to talk to me, to look at me, to tell me I am lazy or worthless or –

You are behind me.

I could slot into you, and I know this because two hours ago, by the open window, you pulled me into your chest and we danced, just for a moment.

But I open the door, and Sam and Josh are there, right there, holding out a bottle of wine.

You didn't want them to come, but Josh was insistent, and I couldn't tell if I was relieved or annoyed.

A flurry of hellos.

Sam hugs me for half a second then lets go.

I take their coats and I drop Sam's by accident.

'Sorry,' I say.

You open the bottle they brought, and it pops, and we clap our hands together and cheer.

Sam spills a little on the floor.

I mop it up.

You hand me paper towels while she sits there, apologising.

The oven timer goes off and I go to check it.

Josh follows me into the kitchen and I wish –

I feel your eyes on my back.

I take the tray out and he leans against the fridge.

He doesn't say anything, just watches me.

'What?'

'Are you okay?' he says, low, conspiratorial.

If I stay here, I will –

'You just look a bit stressed. Can I help with anything?'

I hand him the plates and ask him to lay the table.

You pass him on the way in.

'Sam needs a coaster,' you say.

Josh smiles at you but looks at the floor as he leaves.

I stick a skewer in the meat.

You poke me in the side and it could almost be playful.

The juices run pink.

'Five more minutes.' My voice light.

You reach out and take my wrist, and you kiss me.

I feel your teeth on my lip and I pull away and wipe my mouth.

'Oh, sorry,' Sam says in the doorway.

We move apart.

My lip stings.

'Can I help?'

'Coaster.' You hand it to her.

'Thanks,' she says, looking at me.

'Out in a minute,' I say, and she nods.

Later, they will leave, and we will wave them out the door, and five minutes after that you will fling the dish at the wall next to my head, casually, so casually, and I'll gasp and my lungs will fill with exquisite air, and then I will spend half an hour cleaning gravy out of the carpet, and the next day, I will find pieces of ceramic in my hair.

If I stay here –

I will –

'

The doorbell rings and I open it, and you are behind me, and I can feel your breath on my neck, and my face is red from where I have spent the last ten minutes asking you –

'Hello,' I say. 'It's so nice to see you.'

They give me their coats, and I take Sam's and don't drop it, and I pull her close and hug her tightly and she wraps her arms around my back.

I show them around, and I laugh at Josh's jokes.

I take your hand.

You still don't look at me, but it's alright, you know I'm trying.

The cork pops and we all clap and cheer, me loudest of all.

Sam almost spills her wine, but I catch it before it falls.

Josh applauds and I smile and hand Sam a coaster and she thanks me.

You don't.

You are –

I go into the kitchen to check on the meat, and Josh begins to follow me, and I say loudly, 'No don't worry, just relax,' and he does so, obediently.

You linger in the doorway, not saying anything.

I pass you on the way to find the skewer, and I press my hand to your cheek.

The meat is tender and perfect.

You poke me in the side in a way that is almost playful and I spin around and reach up and kiss you.

We eat and drink and laugh, and the light and music spill through the open window to the street below, and then they leave, and you throw the dish at the wall next to my head, not at my head, exactly, but the brick and plaster next to it, and then I spend the next day picking ceramic out of my hair.

'

Doorbell.

Me, with my face red, you –

Sam embarrassed –

Me too –

Josh flushed and stupid after a single drink.

You behind me –

Always behind me.

They give me their coats and I let them fall to the floor –

No one notices.

Might as well be –

If I stay here –

Josh kisses me on the cheek and I turn my head so it catches the side of my lip.

'Oh,' he says, just so he can say something.

You behind me –

If I –

I realise that I have turned to stone, but nobody seems to notice.

Sam spills her wine.

I slice her palm with the corkscrew and she bleeds into the stain –

If I don't leave, I will –

I twist the skewer in the meat.

You are behind me, and you poke me, and it's almost playful, but I know it's not.

I know it's not.

I know it's not.

I could do it.

Believe me.

You reach out and take my waist and I turn around and I stick the skewer between your ribs.

'

Your eyes blow out.

And you exhale like you're disappointed in me.

Blood blooms on your shirt.

Your lovely shirt.

I bought that shirt for you, with your money.

You blink at me, and your eyes are going liquid.

Massive, dripping pools.

Goodbye, I think.

My God.

Thank God.

+

Anyway, you're the one who leaves me in the end.

Another disappointment.

One day, you come home, and you tell me you're leaving because you're in love with someone else.

And that makes me feel –

'

I mean, it's extraordinary.

The first thing I feel is –

You tell me as I'm sitting on the floor, folding underwear.

You stand in the door, legs wide, arms crossed.

You look ridiculous.

I wish I could tell you.

I suppose I could.

'Who is she?'

'Does it really matter?'

Yes.

'No, I guess not.'

'Take your time with moving.'

'Obviously I wasn't planning on staying,' I say, and I think you'll walk off, but you don't, you just fold your arms and look at the ceiling.

'I'm glad you're being an adult about this.'

Who is she?

It doesn't matter.

'Who is she?'

You look at me like I'm insane.

'Does she know?'

'What?' You sound genuinely at a loss.

I can feel myself starting to smile.

'Does she know what kind of person you are?'

You roll your eyes. Why not humour me? 'Go on. What kind of person am I?'

'

I say it.

'

It sounds wrong.

Your hand goes to your cheek.

'You hit me,' you say. 'Here. You hit me.'

I was there too, I want to say.

I'll remember everything.

You look at me, and your eyes are glassy. 'You're lucky. To have found someone who loved you like me.'

I place your folded laundry into the basket. 'Okay.'

+

I sit in my childhood bedroom.

It stinks of cooking oil.

I come home from work and I sit on the floor and I count how much money I owe you.

My mum watches me in the mornings, stirring instant coffee into a mug I painted when I was ten.

'What happened?'

'Nothing,' I say. 'It didn't work out.'

She squeezes her eyes shut. Massages her temples.

'He left you.'

'No. Yes, I guess.'

She shakes her head.

'He was a good man. You would have been happy together.'

She believes it. She really does.

'What did you do?' she says.

'

'Nothing,' I say.

+

Sam takes me on holiday with her.

Josh gives me a clumsy kiss on the forehead before we drive off.

I pat him on the arm.

'Thanks,' I say into the air.

He shakes his head at nothing.

'We don't have to talk about it if you don't want to,' Sam says matter of factly as I climb into the car.

I want to cut it open and pull out the entrails.

Run it through my hands, red and steaming.

Halfway down the M4, I say, 'Did you know?'

She grips the steering wheel.

'No. But.' She blinks twice and I realise she's trying not to cry. 'I introduced you. It's my fault. I'm sorry.'

The tears fall onto her cheeks, and I start to laugh.

She glares at me, face turning red. 'Don't laugh at me.'

I give her a tissue.

'We're on a motorway,' she says, flapping her hand.

I dab her eyes for her.

And I say: 'I hit him. In the face. Hard.'

She looks at me sideways. 'Okay.'

It starts to rain, and she leans forward, squinting through the windshield.

Suddenly: 'Can you report him?'

And say what? I think.

'I'm tired,' I say instead.

She looks away.

'But.'

'What?'

There is such pity in her face it makes me want to –

'Nina. What if he does it again?'

'

We go to a cottage by the sea.

I am consumed with chopping vegetables as small as they will go.

I let the pot simmer, and after a while, there is nothing else to do.

I sit down at the table and I drink a glass of water.

And I think –

I am not happy, but –

I think I could live like this.

I think I could live with this kind of loneliness.

I don't think I would be happy, but I don't think it would kill me, either.

Maybe that's what life is.

What my life will be.

I hope it isn't, but if it is –

I think it would be okay.

I think that life would still be liveable, that way.

And then the pot boils over, and Sam comes back into the house, shaking water off her raincoat.

'I have to tell you something,' she says, taking her shoes off. 'I wanted to think about the right way to tell you.'

I ask her if she's engaged and she laughs and it turns into a sob.

She holds her stomach.

'Oh,' I say. 'Congratulations.'

'I didn't know how to tell you. I'm sorry.'

She reaches out for me, and I hug her, and for the first time since, I nearly cry.

+

Part of me feels unmoored without Gabriel.

But it all goes on.

It shocks me, sometimes.

I walk through the park with Sam, my hand in her coat pocket.

I try to sleep with a man I meet on an app, but I can't, so I leave.

Adam gets headhunted, and my new boss mostly ignores me.

I have nightmares, and I crawl into my mum's bed.

A GP prescribes me sertraline, but it makes me tired, so I stop taking it.

I stop drinking for a while. It makes me itchy.

He never asks for it, but I send him his money back in tiny monthly instalments.

I answer the phone at the restaurant, and I bag the takeaway orders with my father.

Chris and I smoke in the alleyway.

'

I never see him again.

I feel like I should, like I should glimpse the back of his head in a supermarket while I'm buying fabric softener, but I don't.

I just don't.

+

I go out early one morning, before dawn.

I walk into the centre of the city.

And I see a man crying.

He is wearing a suit and tie, slightly crooked.

He looks a little younger than my father.

He sits, splay-legged on the side of the street.

I've never seen an adult cry like this.

Like a child, with their whole body, like they're going to snap in half from the force of it.

I watch him, and he sees me watching him, but he doesn't stop.

I cross the road and he looks up.

I sit down, and I reach out and take his arm.

He shudders.

And after a moment, he places his hand on top of mine.

End.

www.ingramcontent.com/pod-product-compliance
Ingram Content Group UK Ltd.
Pitfield, Milton Keynes, MK11 3LW, UK
UKHW02707280225
455688UK00012B/307